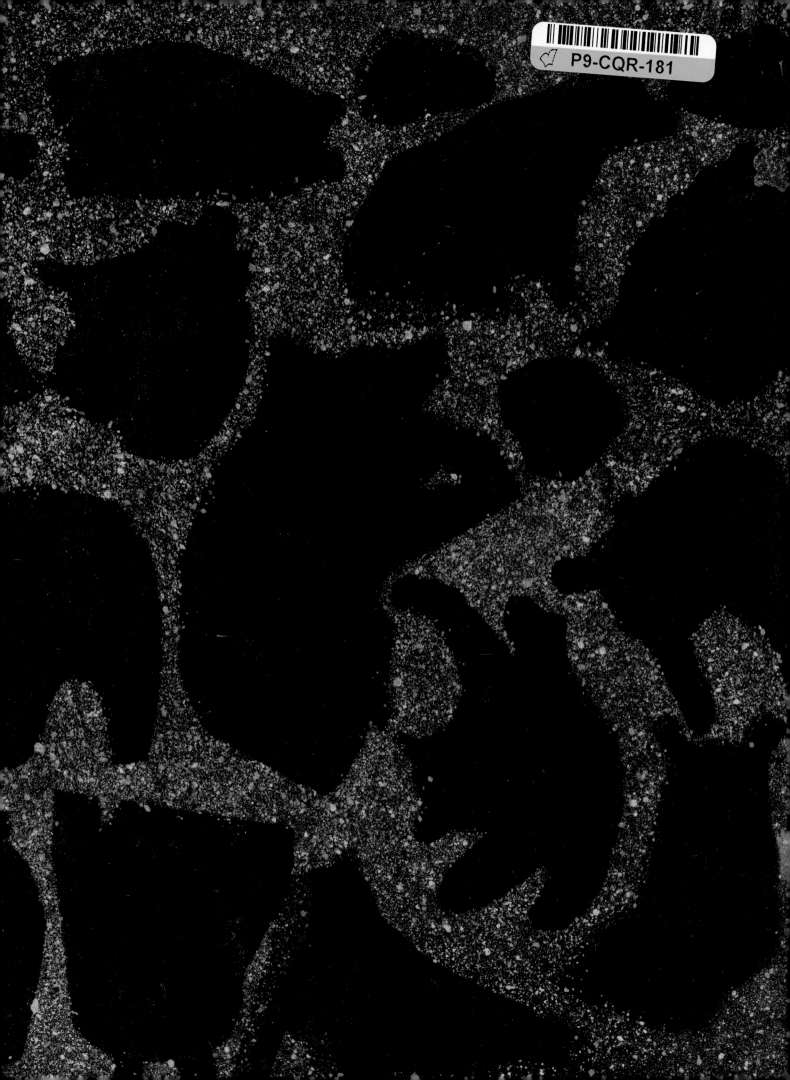

To Jill Robinson and all those
working so hard for the moon bears
—B. Z. G.

To Integrity, "the Spiritual Bear,"
so we may reclaim green humanity
lost to unharnessed "wants" disguised as our needs
—E. Y.

Thanks to Laura Godwin, Noa Wheeler, Patrick Collins, Tim Jones,
Eileen Lawrence, Caroline Sun, Karen Frangipane, George Wen, Judy Sisko,
Jennifer Doerr, and all those at Holt who helped with this book.

Henry Holt and Company, LLC, *Publishers since 1866*
175 Fifth Avenue, New York, New York 10010 [www.HenryHoltKids.com]

Library of Congress Cataloging-in-Publication Data
Guiberson, Brenda Z.
Moon bear / Brenda Z. Guiberson ; pictures by Ed Young.
p.   cm.
ISBN 978-0-8050-8977-6
1. Asiatic black bear—Juvenile literature. I. Young, Ed, ill. II. Title.
QL737.C27G834 2010   599.78—dc22   2009017931

First Edition—2010 / Designed by Patrick Collins
Printed in March 2010 in China by Toppan Leefung Printing Ltd.,
Dongguan City, Guangdong Province, on acid-free paper. ∞

10 9 8 7 6 5 4 3 2

A portion of the proceeds from this book will be donated to Animals Asia Foundation Ltd.,
a California nonprofit public benefit corporation, dedicated to improving the lives of moon
bears and all animals in Asia, ending cruelty, and restoring respect for animals Asia-wide.
For more information contact Animals Asia Foundation Ltd., 300 Broadway, Suite 32,
San Francisco, CA 94133-4587 [www. animalsasia.org]. This contribution is not tax deductible.

Moon Bear

Brenda Z. Guiberson

illustrated by Ed Young

Henry Holt and Company

New York

Who blinks in the sunlight
that peeks through the Himalayas?

Sleepy moon bear,
waking up
from a long winter snooze.

Who scratches the birch tree
and licks oozing sap?

Hungry moon bear,
slurping sweetness
after months without food.

Who claws the tree trunks
in the rhododendron forest?

Cautious moon bear,
marking her territory.

Who searches for new shoots
of the fast-growing bamboo?

Bold moon bear,
munching near the red panda.

Who scritches and shuffles
through soggy leaf litter?

Curious moon bear,
licking up ants
after the drenching monsoon.

Who plucks raspberries
and plops red scat in the tangle?

*Blissful moon bear,
feasting on juicy summer fruit.*

Who scuttles up the tree
and bends back the branches?

Clever moon bear,
gulping cherries
before the barking deer below.

Who tries to sleep
in the nest of broken limbs?

Grumpy moon bear,
swatting insects
in the steamy summer sizzle.

Who climbs to the snow
in the high Himalayas?

Wandering moon bear,
walking upright
and sniffing for marmots.

Who zigzags to the lowlands,
avoiding poachers and loggers?

Adventurous moon bear,
looking for any good meal to eat.

Who gulps the fall crops
of beechnuts and acorns?

Happy moon bear,
gorging on extra food
for the winter.

Who digs into a tree hollow
and adds a carpet of ferns?

Chubby moon bear,
snuggling in for another
long winter snooze.

Who shuffles out in spring
so hungry again?

Mama moon bear!

And baby moon bears too.
Grrrr! Grrrowl! Grifff!

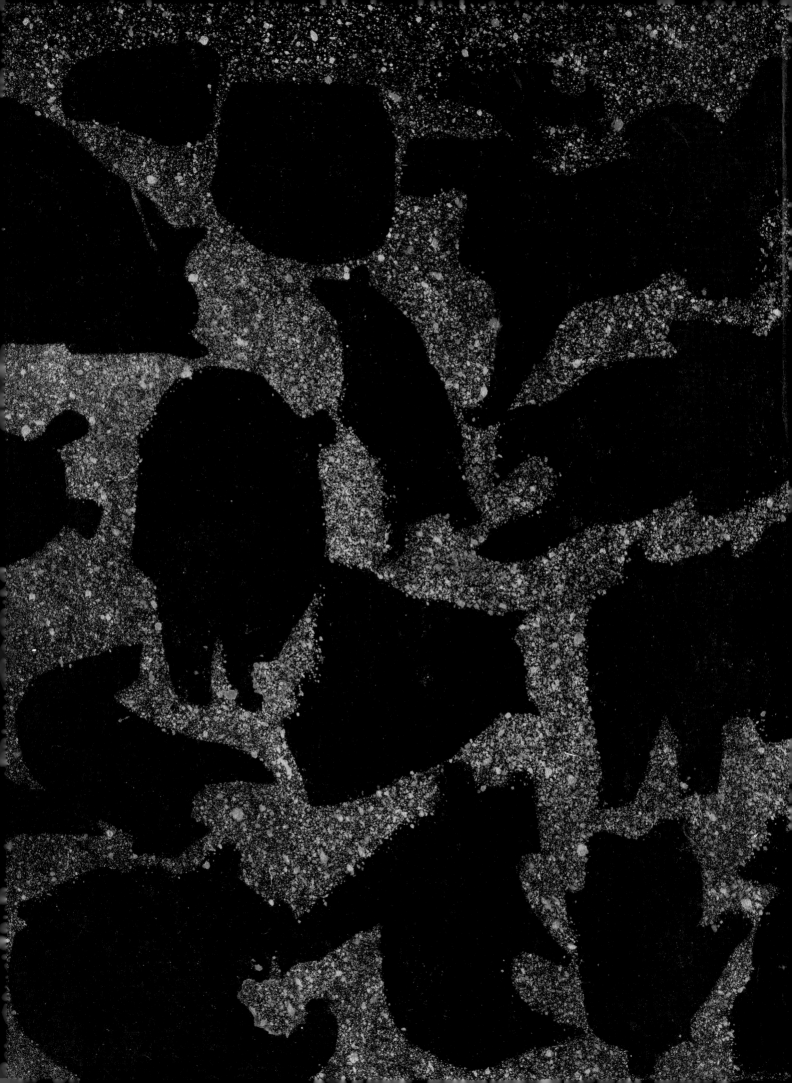